UNEARTH 21 TECHNIQUES TO TRANSFORM SELF-DOUBTS INTO GROWTH

DIVE DEEP INTO THE OCEAN OF INTROSPECTION

CHITRA JAISWAL

Made with ♥ on the Notion Press Platform
www.notionpress.com

This book is dedicated to three cherished couples who are the pillars of my life.

First, to the couple who brought me into this world. No matter what I give them, it will never be enough to repay their immense love and support. This dedication is just a small token of my gratitude.

Next, to my elder brother and sister-in-law. My brother has always been a father figure to me, always ready to fulfill my wishes, except when my stubbornness gets the best of me.

And finally, to my elder sister and brother-in-law. We've adopted each other as family—I've become their first child, and they have become my parents and my children.

These three couples are the anchors of my life. With them by my side, I feel protected and loved. This dedication is my humble attempt to give back a little of the endless love they've showered me with.

Me with The Pillars of my Foundation

Contents

Preface

A loop of worrying about others' opinions is always surrounded around us. In this process, we fail to recognize that the loudest criticisms and doubts often come from within. We tend to reject our own thoughts, passions, and dreams, fearing disapproval from others. Before anyone else can criticize us, we become our own harshest critics.

I recently came to a profound realization: before seeking love and support from others, I need to accept, support, and love myself. When you truly love yourself, you unlock a powerful charm and confidence. This confident charisma naturally attracts attention and support from others. Initially, people may feel envy or denial towards you, but when they see that their opinions do not shake your confidence, they start to praise you and recognize your potential—potential that remains undimmed by self-doubt and external opinions.

This realization gave me the impulse to dive deep into introspection and transform my self-doubts into pillars of growth. Today, I am transformed and charismatic, and I owe this transformation to the techniques I am about to share with you in this book. Each technique has been self-implemented and has played a crucial role in my journey of self-discovery and growth.

While writing this book, self-doubts occasionally resurfaced. I questioned whether the techniques I discovered would be relevant to your life, as everyone's doubts are different. However, I silenced these doubts with the conviction that, although our doubts may vary, the techniques will be universally relevant if you master the art of self-introspection.

In the chapters that follow, you will find 21 techniques designed to help you transform your self-doubts into opportunities for growth. As you read through these pages, I hope you will find the inspiration and tools you need to embark on your own journey of self-acceptance and transformation. Let these techniques guide you as they have guided me, and may you emerge confident, charismatic, and ready to embrace the support and praise that will naturally come your way.

Acknowledgements

First and foremost, I want to express my deepest gratitude to the ultimate supremacy, the divine power, "God". In moments of doubt and uncertainty, your presence has provided me with the courage and faith to continue and illuminated my path of self-introspection. I am also extremely thankful to myself. This journey of introspection has been a profound and transformative experience. It has required immense courage and honesty to face my own doubts and fears, and I am grateful for the strength and resilience I discovered within myself.

To my family, your unwavering support and love have been my anchor. Thank you for believing in me even when I doubted myself. Your encouragement has been a source of constant strength, and I am forever grateful for your presence in my life.

To my friends, your companionship and understanding have made this journey more bearable. Thank you for listening, for your kind words, and for reminding me of my worth when I needed it the most. Your friendship has been a beacon of light in my darkest moments.

To the readers of this book, thank you for embarking on this journey with me. Your willingness to explore and transform your own self-doubts is a testament to your courage and strength. I hope that the techniques shared in this book will be as transformative for you as they have been for me.

Lastly, I want to acknowledge everyone who has played a part, no matter how small, in the creation of this book. Your contributions, support, and encouragement have made this possible, and I am deeply grateful.

With heartfelt thanks,
Chitra Jaiswal

About The Author

Chitra Jaiswal

(Author)

Chitra Jaiswal stands out with her unique talent and promise. She has a background in commerce and works as a Company Secretary. Chitra is also a published author, with her first book being "Eternal Love-Can Happen Twice?". She continued to captivate readers with other books like "From Foes to Flames", "Shades in Pairs: Tangled Threads of Life," and "The Echoing Algorithm," and has co-authored over 20 anthologies. Besides her corporate career, she loves writing poems and articles, a passion she's had since 2018. She shares her work on her Facebook page "Soch Ka Sauch" and her blog "Swach Soch."

Chitra blends her business knowledge with her artistic skills, connecting deeply with her readers. Her writing offers a fresh and inspiring perspective. Apart from the passion of writing, she loves to dance, listen to music and spending time with family and friends. She is an extremist and empathetic human being. She believes that her first duty is towards the society as a whole. Her life's goal is to make the world a better place to live in and restore the humanity in the world by impacting the lives of many.

Let's Follow her on Social Media:

Website: https://sites.google.com/view/scribblesofchitra/home

BlogSpot: https://swachsoch.blogspot.com

Facebook Page: https://www.facebook.com/sochswachsoch

Instagram: https://www.instagram.com/scribbles_of_chitra

CHAPTER ONE

INTRODUCTION

Let's first give you the insight on what it is all about "The art of Introspection". The art of introspection refers to the practice of self-examination and reflection on one's own thoughts, feelings, and behaviors. It involves looking inward to gain a deeper understanding of oneself, including one's motivations, desires, strengths, and weaknesses. This process can lead to greater self-awareness, personal growth, and emotional intelligence.

Have you ever really looked at your body? Every part is unique, even those in pairs. Take your fingers, for example—each one is different. Your hands aren't identical; one might be slightly thinner or weaker in strength than the other. The same goes for your legs, eyes, and every other part of you. This is normal, isn't it? So, how can anyone expect everyone to be the same? Each person has their own strengths and unique traits, and that's exactly how it should be. We are not here to be replica of others, are we?

Why the art of introspection is essential for growth? Let's dig deep, we all experience self-doubt. It's not just an occasional feeling; it's something we face every moment. Humans are often their own harshest critics. Our destructive thoughts can be more powerful than our constructive ones. We come up with countless reasons why we didn't do something we wanted to, but deep down, we know these are just excuses. The most significant barrier to achieving our dreams is often our own selves. We let our inner demons of self-doubt win and overpower us.

Have you ever taken the time to really look at your actions and yourself? The questions that have stopped you or the actions that went wrong have answers and alternatives within them. If you can master the art of self-introspection and commit to improving yourself each day, you will transform your vision of life. You will find perspective and purpose.

You might be wondering: if everyone is unique, how can these techniques work for everyone? Let's clear that up before we begin our journey. While we each have our own strengths and traits, deep down, we're all social beings who seek emotional support, love, peace, and acceptance. Our need for mental and emotional peace is not a weakness. In fact, it's one of the greatest gifts we can give and receive.

We often feel misunderstood, thinking no one truly gets us. But do we really understand ourselves? People say they want to be rich, own a house, or enjoy luxurious comforts. Yet, behind these material goals lies a deeper desire: to be respected, to make others proud or even envious, to feel wanted, loved, accepted, and understood. When we can't find this emotional comfort, we seek power or authority over others, hoping they'll do as we say, even if it's out of fear or greed.

Ultimately, we want to be accepted for who we are, but often, we don't even accept ourselves. Can you relate to this? If not, maybe you haven't looked deeply enough into your own feelings and desires. Maybe you haven't truly found yourself yet.

Each person on this earth has a unique purpose. We are not here just to follow a cycle of sleep, wake, eat, and repeat. Are we? Are you ready to join me on this journey of transforming self-doubt into pillars of growth? Let's dive into this deep ocean of introspection and unearth the techniques for this transformation. Turn the page to discover the first technique. With each page, I hope a single candle will transform into the blazing sun. Are you ready to be my scuba partner? Fasten your scuba suit and kit and let's dive deep together into the ocean of self-introspection.

CHAPTER TWO

Scuba Dooby Doo

When we talk about diving deep into the ocean of introspection, we need to start with the basics. Think of it like learning to scuba dive. First, train your brain to introspect, not overthink. Begin by understanding yourself.

Plan Your Dive:

Just like scuba diving, introspection requires a plan. Your conscious and subconscious mind are your diving buddies, and together, they have all the answers. Take time to sync them up and match their pace. Remember, it's a continuous process, but you need to take breaks. Don't dive so deep that you forget to enjoy the present moment. Know your limits—introspection has boundaries unlike overthinking.

Check Your Equipment:

Before diving in, make sure your heart and mind are aligned. These two often contradict, so clear your thoughts and align your conscience.

Ascend Slowly and Safely:

Don't rush. Everything gets better and wiser with time. Mastering introspection, like any art, requires patience.

Equalize Early and Often:

Balance your introspection with your self-doubts. Whenever doubts arise, take a moment to introspect and find clarity.

Know Your Limits:

Understand your emotional and mental boundaries. Everyone has different limits, so don't compare yourself to others.

Know Your Surroundings:

Identify your safe places and people. Gather perspectives from others, but don't follow them blindly. Use these insights to help your subconscious find its own answers.

With each chapter, you'll get closer to mastering the art of introspection using my proven techniques and examples. Don't worry—with time and practice, you'll become a pro at diving deep into your inner self and transforming your self-doubts into growth.

CHAPTER THREE

TREAT YOURSELF WITH A LITTLE RETREAT

Sometimes, we forget to talk to the most important person in our lives: ourselves. Taking a step back from the world to spend time with yourself can be the best gift you can give. I often take these moments to reflect, introspect, and analyze my thoughts and feelings. As a writer, this time allows me to explore my mind and put my thoughts into words, crafting them into phrases or poems.

During these retreat periods, I often discover my short-term and long-term goals, what I want to achieve, and what experiences I desire before I die. Recently, I challenged myself to write every day for 30 days. This challenge helped me introspect and gain clarity about my desires, self-doubts, inner demons, and vulnerabilities. During these 30 days, I shared my poems on social media, realizing through this process that I am ready for true love and a life partner. More than a third of my poems were about my expectations for a partner, while others reflected on self-reflection, the darkness in the world, and spirituality, as I am a devotee of Shiva. My poems often dedicated to Him while exploring my spiritual journey.

My manifestation of love was so clear that people began to ask if I was in love. Although I am an old-fashioned girl who doesn't easily share her feelings, this challenge made me realize my expectations for a future partner. I discovered that I am an extremist in relationships, pouring my soul into them, whether it's friendship or family. I am not interested in materialistic love but seek a deep, hard-to-find kind of love. I crave the same love I give to others. There were times during this journey when I felt vulnerable, but I recovered without anyone's support through introspection. I used to think I had no expectations from people, but I was wrong and was in denial with the fact. Accepting this truth helped me understand that having expectations is normal and reflects our emotional needs.

The first step in introspection is accepting that you have some expectations from yourself, your loved ones, and the world. Climb out of the denial phase. You can grow when you accept the benefits and shortcomings of your expectations.

Let's plan the first level of introspection. The methods listed here are inclusive, not exhaustive:

Creating the Environment:

Find a comfortable environment for introspection. For me, it's nighttime when the world is quiet, and my inner voice is loudest. Sometimes, when an incident affect me deeply, it lingers in my subconscious mind, even in a busy schedule. Then, I decide to reflect on my expectations from that situation and how to solve it. Your environment could be a nature walk, listening to music, or anything that helps you connect with your inner self.

Journaling:

Journaling helps you understand your expectations. Summarize incidents and jot down your thoughts. This process helps you identify expectations from situations or people.

Art Therapy:

Art therapy is a great way to explore your mind. Every person has an artistic side, even if they don't realize it. Find what excites you or brings you peace, and use it as your art form. Remember, art therapy is not a competition; it's about reflecting your situation in your art. You don't need to be perfect and canvas your masterpiece.

Self-Compassionate Exercise:

Put yourself in the shoes of a compassionate friend and write a letter to yourself. This exercise will help you understand your expectations and emotional needs.

Reflective Reading:

Incorporate reading into your daily routine. It could be anything you enjoy, like a comic or a picture book. Reflective reading helps you be more mindful of yourself.

Gratitude Practice:

Practice gratitude daily. Everyone has something others don't, and it's important to appreciate what you have. Gratitude attracts positivity and should be a part of your daily routine.

Other Must Practices:

Set a daily timer for self-reflection. Avoid distractions like phones and social media. Be gentle with yourself; the world is already harsh enough. Approach your reflections with kindness and self-compassion. Adjust your schedule based on how you feel and what you need. Spend some time in silence each day to deepen your reflections.

There are no strict rules. These practices are effective for me, but you can skip any that don't resonate with you. Now, let's move on to our next chapter.

CHAPTER FOUR

MIRROR, MIRROR!

Now that we have accept that we have some expectations with the world, before we dive deeper into understanding ourselves, let's take a moment to embrace our expectations. Understanding and clarity of our expectations helps us set clear goals and navigate our paths with purpose.

As we reflect on our lives, we must first recognize what we truly expect from ourselves and from life. We must ask ourselves, "What do we want to achieve?" and "Why do we hold these expectations?"

This chapter is about identifying those expectations and preparing ourselves to meet them. It's a journey of self-discovery that requires honesty and introspection.

I believe in the philosophy that to understand others, we must first understand ourselves. This mirrors my quote: "Whenever you pick up a mirror, first reflect on yourself before others."

To make meaningful connections with others, we need to know who we are and what we stand for. By spending time understanding ourselves, we can then give the best of ourselves to others.

To help you on this journey, I have created a list of reflection questions. These questions have guided me in my own self-reflection and personal growth. Remember, it's okay if you don't have all the answers right away. The goal is to start thinking deeply about yourself and your life. You deserve this time to focus on you.

Reflection Questions

1. What are your core beliefs and values?

- Think about the beliefs and values that guide your decisions. What values are non-negotiable for you?

2. What are your greatest strengths and weaknesses?

- Identify your strengths and weaknesses for improvement. How can you grow?

3. What is coping mechanism from stress and adversity?

- Think about your coping mechanism and how you react in difficult situations. Are they healthy and effective?

4. What achievements are you most proud of and how do you celebrate them?

- Celebrate your achievements. What makes you feel proud and satisfied and how do you recognize these successes?

5. What failures taught you the most valuable lessons?

- Reflect on the lessons of your life through your past experiences. How have these experiences shaped you?

6. How do you define success and happiness?

- Define what success and happiness means to you. How do these definitions guide your goals?

7. What are your short-term and long-term goals, and how do you measure progress toward them?

- Set clear and achievable goals. What are your goals- the short and long term? How do you track and celebrate your progress?

8. What motivates and inspires you?

- Identify your source of motivation. What drives you to pursue your goals?

9. What fears prevent you from realizing your full potential and how do you deal with them?

- Accept your fear. How do they affect your ability to achieve your dreams and how do you deal with them?

10. How adaptable you are with change and uncertainty?

- Consider your adaptability. How do you react to new or unpredictable situations?

11. What does your ideal life look like?

- Imagine your perfect life. What would make you happy and fulfilled?

12. What does balance mean to you and how do you maintain it?

- Balance is the key to well-being. How do you juggle different aspects of your life?

13. What are your passions and interests and how do you spend your free time?

- Determine what you like to do. Do your leisure activities reflect your values and interests?

14. Which human relationships are most important to you and how do you value them?

- Think about the people in your life. Who is most important to you and how do you invest in those relationships?

15. How do you show love and appreciation to others?

- Think about how you express affection and gratitude. How do you make others feel valued?

16. How do you resolve conflicts and disagreements?

- Consider your approach to conflict resolution. Is it efficient and respectful?

17. What limits do you put on your relationships?

- Health limits are critical. How do you protect your well-being when interacting with others?

18. How do you express your feelings?

- Consider your emotional expression. Can you express your feelings clearly and constructively?

19. What habits and routines boost your well-being?

- Identify your healthy habits. What routines support your physical, mental and emotional health?

20. How do you take care of your physical, mental and emotional health?

- Think about your self-care practices. What do you do to stay healthy and balanced?

21. What role does spirituality play in your life?

- Consider your spiritual beliefs and practices. How do they affect your life?

22. What are your favorite ways to practice self-care?

- Self-care is essential. What activities help you relax and recharge?

23. How do you stay focused and productive and what are the biggest distractions in your life?

- Determine your productivity strategy. What helps you stay on track with your tasks and goals? What interrupts your focus and how can you minimize these distractions?

24. How do you manage your time effectively?

- Think about your time management skills. How do you prioritize and plan your activities?

25. What activities help you relax?

- Consider your relaxation techniques. What helps you relax and rejuvenate?

26. How to maintain motivation in difficult times?

- Identify the sources of your stamina. What keeps you going when things get tough?

Each of these questions provides a pathway to deeper self-understanding. Embrace the process with an open heart and mind, and let these reflections guide you towards a more fulfilled and authentic life. As you ponder these questions, you may find answers that surprise you or challenge you to think differently. Remember, this is your time to focus on you and your growth.

Now that we've explored our expectations and begun the process of self-reflection, it's time to dive deeper into discovering who we truly are. Let's continue this journey of self-introspection.

CHAPTER FIVE

FOMO!

Now that we have shown ourselves a mirror and have been honestly reflective ourselves to ourselves. In the process, you must have found some hidden inner ghosts which are the reasons of your discomfort. The one among the major discomforts is “FOMO”. Is it resonating?

Understanding FOMO: The Basics

FOMO, or the "Fear of Missing Out," is a pervasive psychological phenomenon that manifests as the anxiety that others are having rewarding experiences from which one is absent. This fear is often intensified by social media, where curated snapshots of others’ lives create an illusion of constant fun and success. FOMO can lead to a persistent feeling of inadequacy, as individuals compare their own lives unfavorably with the highlight reels of others.

The Problem with FOMO

FOMO can have significant negative impacts on mental health and well-being. Here are some of the primary issues associated with it:

1. **Increased Anxiety and Stress:** Constantly worrying about missing out on experiences can lead to chronic stress and anxiety. This is often accompanied by feelings of inadequacy and low self-esteem, as individuals feel they are not living up to the exciting lives they perceive others to have.

2. **Reduced Life Satisfaction:** Focusing on what others are doing instead of appreciating one’s own life can diminish overall life satisfaction. People with high levels of FOMO often struggle to enjoy their present moments, as they are preoccupied with what they might be missing out on.

3. **Impaired Decision-Making:** FOMO can lead to impulsive decision-making and a lack of commitment. Individuals might constantly change plans or commitments in fear of missing out on something better, leading to a lack of focus and direction.

4. **Social Media Addiction:** The relentless checking of social media feeds to stay updated on others' activities can become an addiction. This can interfere with daily life, productivity, and real-life social interactions.

Overcoming FOMO involves transforming the underlying self-doubt into a path for personal growth. Using the right techniques, one can achieve this transformation through self-introspection.

The Cultural Context of FOMO

In today's culture, especially among Gen Z, FOMO has become a trendy term, almost a style statement. People share their FOMO experiences on social media to reach a wider audience and gain popularity. However, this often masks the real issues, underlying FOMO. The desire for popularity, fame, money, power, and authority drives many to chase after these fears blindly, often forgetting their core values in the process.

The Real Demons

The real demons of FOMO are hidden beneath the surface. Humans have a tendency to be influenced by influential people, which drives the desire to feel authority over others. However, the true needs of humans are attention, love, care, support, and peace. Self-love is the first step to eradicating these demons. Everyone is the star of their own story, yet we often cast ourselves as supporting characters or even the villains in our own narratives. This resonates with many, reflecting the self-deterioration caused by FOMO.

Social Media Addiction

Social media addiction exacerbates FOMO. Many of us start our day by checking our phones, which diminishes self-esteem and is a significant contributor to FOMO. Recognizing this habit is crucial for overcoming FOMO and rebuilding self-worth.

FOMO is a significant challenge in the modern, interconnected world, but it is possible to transform this fear into a catalyst for personal growth.

By understanding the roots of FOMO, setting realistic goals, practicing gratitude, reframing negative thoughts, seeking support, limiting social media use, and embracing the present moment, you can overcome self-doubt and foster a more fulfilling and authentic life. This journey of introspection not only helps in conquering FOMO but also paves the way for continuous personal growth and self-improvement.

CHAPTER SIX

IT'S OK TO NOT TO BE OK!

The world often demands perfection, it's easy to feel overwhelmed. Society tells us to smile through pain, to always be productive, and to hide our struggles. But what if we took a step back and acknowledged that it's okay to not to be okay? What if we embraced our vulnerabilities, understanding that we are human and it is natural? This chapter explores the profound importance of accepting our imperfections, recognizing our emotional struggles, and finding strength in our vulnerabilities.

Embracing Imperfections

As we have already resonated with the fact that our physical landscapes are unique and it's a constant to change.

Similarly, our emotional landscapes are diverse and varied. No two people experience the world in the same way, and that's a beautiful thing. Our struggles and imperfections make us who we are. The valuable lessons learnt through these experiences have shaped us. Embracing our imperfections means acknowledging that we don't have to be perfect to be worthy of love, respect, and happiness.

The Myth of Perfection

Perfection is an illusion, a myth that we often chase without realizing it's unattainable. Society bombards us with images of flawless beauty, success, and happiness. Social media feeds are filled with curated moments that rarely reflect reality. It's easy to fall into the trap of comparing ourselves to these unrealistic standards, feeling inadequate and unworthy as a result.

Perfection is a myth, it doesn't exist. Everyone has flaws, insecurities, and moments of doubt. By embracing our imperfections, we can let go of the unrealistic expectations we place on ourselves and others. We can start to see beauty in our flaws and strength in our vulnerabilities.

The Power of Vulnerability

Vulnerability is frequently perceived as a flaw, something to conceal or surmount. But in reality, vulnerability is a powerful force. It's through our vulnerabilities that we connect with others on a deeper level. When we embrace vulnerability, we pave the way for authentic connections and profound relationships.

A renowned researcher on vulnerability, explains that vulnerability is the birthplace of creativity, innovation, and change. By embracing our vulnerabilities, we can tap into our true potential and live more authentic lives. It's okay to admit that we're not okay. It's okay to seek help and support when we need it. In doing so, we find strength in our vulnerability and resilience in our struggles.

Recognizing Emotional Struggles

Life is a rollercoaster of emotions. There are times of joy and celebration, but there are also moments of sadness, anxiety, and despair. Recognizing and acknowledging our emotional struggles is an essential step in our journey toward healing and self-acceptance.

The Stigma of Mental Health

Despite progress in recent years, mental health still carries a significant stigma. Many people feel ashamed or embarrassed to talk about their emotional struggles. They fear judgment, rejection, or being perceived as weak. This stigma prevents individuals from seeking the help they need and deserve.

It's essential to recognize that mental well-being holds equal significance to physical health. Just as we wouldn't hesitate to seek medical help for a physical ailment, we shouldn't hesitate to seek support for our mental and emotional well-being. It's perfectly alright to not feel okay, and it's absolutely fine to seek help when you need it.

The Importance of Self-Awareness

Self-awareness is the key to recognizing our emotional struggles. It involves tuning into our thoughts, feelings, and behaviors, and understanding how they impact our well-being. Self-awareness allows us to identify when we're not okay and take proactive steps to address our needs.

Practicing mindfulness is one way to cultivate self-awareness. Mindfulness is the practice of staying fully engaged in the present, attentively noticing our thoughts and emotions without passing any judgment. It helps us become more accustomed to our emotional state and recognize when we need to take a step back and care for ourselves.

Seeking Support

We don't have to face our struggles alone. Seeking support from friends, family, or mental health professionals can make a significant difference in our ability to cope with emotional challenges. Talking about our feelings can be incredibly therapeutic, providing a sense of relief and validation. We all need a human diary or several different ones for various aspects of our lives.

If you can't find a nonjudgmental safe space in a friend or family member to be your confidant, a trained therapist can offer that environment. A therapist provides a secure and impartial space to explore your emotions, uncover underlying issues, and develop coping strategies. Seeking help is okay, and prioritizing your mental and emotional well-being is crucial. Professional help is always a good option when your problems feel overwhelming. Remember, it's okay to not to be okay. Seeking therapy doesn't make you crazy. Just like visiting a doctor isn't only for severe illnesses, seeing a psychologist can address even minor issues that aren't improving. If something's not getting better on its own, it's wise to seek proper treatment.

Finding Strength in Vulnerabilities

Our vulnerabilities are not weaknesses; they are sources of strength and resilience. By embracing our vulnerabilities, we can find the courage to face life's challenges and grow stronger in the process.

Being vulnerable requires a tremendous amount of bravery. It means acknowledging our fears, insecurities, and pain. It means opening ourselves up to the possibility of rejection or judgment. But it also means being true to ourselves and living authentically.

When we allow ourselves to be vulnerable, we give others permission to do the same. We create a culture of openness and acceptance, where it's okay to not to be okay. This openness about our vulnerabilities strengthens bonds and nurtures a sense of community. Are you brave enough to reveal your own vulnerabilities?

Building Resilience

Resilience is the capability to recover quickly from difficulties. It's not about dodging challenges, but about confronting them directly and gaining valuable lessons from the experience. Our vulnerabilities play a crucial role in building resilience. They teach us about our strengths and limitations, and they help us develop coping strategies to navigate difficult times.

Resilience doesn't mean we won't experience pain or struggle. It means we have the inner strength to endure and overcome. By embracing our vulnerabilities, we build the resilience needed to navigate life's ups and downs.

The Role of Compassion

Compassion, both for ourselves and others, is essential in embracing our vulnerabilities. Self-compassion means extending the same kindness and understanding to ourselves that we would naturally offer to a friend. It means acknowledging our struggles without judgment and giving ourselves permission to be imperfect.

Compassion for others involves recognizing that everyone has their own battles and offering support without judgment. It means creating a safe space for others to express their vulnerabilities and providing a listening ear and a comforting presence.

Stories of Strength in Vulnerability

Throughout history, many individuals have found strength in their vulnerabilities and inspired others with their courage. Here are a few stories that highlight the power of embracing our struggles:

Story 1: J.K. Rowling

J.K. Rowling, the author of the beloved Harry Potter series, faced numerous challenges before achieving success. She battled depression, financial struggles, and rejection from multiple publishers. Instead of giving up, Rowling embraced her vulnerabilities and poured her emotions into her writing. Her story is a testament to the power of resilience and the strength that can be found in embracing our struggles.

Story 2: Oprah Winfrey

Oprah Winfrey is a media mogul and philanthropist known for her inspiring journey from poverty to success. Throughout her life, Oprah faced numerous adversities, including childhood abuse and discrimination. By embracing her vulnerabilities and sharing her story, Oprah has become a beacon of hope for millions. Her resilience and compassion have made her a powerful advocate for self-acceptance and mental health.

Story 3: Michael Phelps

Michael Phelps, the most decorated Olympian of all time, has been open about his struggles with depression and anxiety. Despite his incredible achievements, Phelps faced mental health challenges that led him to seek help and support. By speaking out about his experiences, Phelps has helped break the stigma surrounding mental health and encouraged others to seek help when they need it.

It's okay to not to be okay. This simple yet profound statement reminds us that we don't have to be perfect to be worthy. Our vulnerabilities are not weaknesses; they are sources of strength and resilience. By embracing our imperfections, recognizing our emotional struggles, and finding strength in our vulnerabilities, we can live more authentic and fulfilling lives.

Keep in mind that you are not walking this path alone. Seek support, practice self-compassion, and embrace your uniqueness. Life's challenges may be daunting, but they also offer opportunities for growth and connection. Embrace the journey, and know that it's okay to not to be okay.

CHAPTER SEVEN

From Past's Prisoner to Present's Pioneer

The human mind is like a maze, often trapping us in our past experiences, regrets, and traumas. We become prisoners of our history, weighed down by past mistakes and missed chances. However, the journey from being a prisoner of the past to a pioneer of the present is not only possible but also transformative. It requires an intricate process of introspection, self-compassion, and a conscious decision to live in the moment. This chapter delves into the path of freeing oneself from past shackles and embracing the present.

Understanding the Ghosts of the Past:

The past holds a significant influence over our present behavior and future aspirations. It shapes our identity, beliefs, and perceptions. However, when we cling to negative experiences or unresolved traumas, we become captives to our history. This is called rumination, involves repeatedly thinking about distressing events, which can lead to heightened anxiety, depression, and a pervasive sense of stagnation.

Psychologists say that dwelling on the past stops us from moving forward. Constantly reliving past mistakes or traumas can prevent us from enjoying the present and planning for the future. This mental burden is like carrying a heavy backpack full of stones – the more we focus on the past, the less energy we have for the present and future growth.

The Magic of Surrender

Forgiveness and acceptance are essential components of letting go of the past. Forgiveness does not mean condoning the actions that hurt us, but rather freeing ourselves from the emotional burden of holding onto resentment. When we forgive others or ourselves, we release the hold that past transgressions have on our psyche, making room for healing and growth.

Acceptance involves acknowledging our past experiences without resistance. It means recognizing that what happened cannot be changed and choosing to focus on what can be controlled – our present actions and attitudes. Acceptance is a liberating process that allows us to live in harmony with our past, rather than in conflict with it.

Unleash yourself from Rigidity:

Unleashing yourself from rigidity is a journey of self-discovery and growth, one that requires patience, perseverance, and an open heart. The first step on this path is to set realistic goals. Defining clear, achievable goals for both your personal and professional life can provide direction and purpose. Start by identifying what truly matters to you and then break these goals into smaller, manageable steps. This approach not only makes the process less overwhelming but also allows you to celebrate each milestone, reinforcing your progress and boosting your confidence along the way.

Next, it's crucial to reframe negative thoughts. Self-doubt and negativity can be crippling, holding you back from reaching your full potential. When such thoughts arise, challenge them by questioning their validity. Replace the negativity with positive affirmations that validate your inherent worth and capabilities. Practicing gratitude can also shift your focus toward the positive aspects of your life, helping you to appreciate what you have and fostering a more optimistic outlook. This shift in mindset can open up new possibilities and pathways that were previously obscured by doubt and fear.

Seeking support is another essential component of this journey. Everyone deserves companionship through life's trials and triumphs. Reach out to friends, family, or even a therapist for support. Sharing your journey with others not only provides encouragement but also offers new perspectives that you might not have considered. The insights and advice from others can be invaluable, helping you to see your situation in a new light and offering strategies to overcome obstacles.

Embracing change is perhaps the most challenging but also the most rewarding part of this process. Embracing change is integral to life's journey, as resisting it often results in frustration and a lack of growth. Instead, learn to accept change as a natural and necessary part of growth. Embrace unfamiliar experiences and opportunities, even when they challenge your comfort zone. Each new experience is a chance to learn more about yourself and to develop new skills and strengths.

Unleashing yourself from rigidity means letting go of the need for control and certainty, and instead, embracing the fluid and dynamic nature of life. It's about being flexible and adaptable, and willing to evolve as circumstances change. By setting realistic goals, reframing negative thoughts, seeking support, and embracing change, you can break free from the constraints of rigidity and open yourself up to a more fulfilling and authentic life.

Remember, this is a journey, not a destination. There will be setbacks and challenges along the way, but each one is an opportunity to learn and grow. Celebrate your progress, no matter how small, and keep moving forward with an open heart and a resilient spirit. By doing so, you will discover a sense of freedom and empowerment that comes from living life on your own terms, and embracing the beauty and unpredictability of the journey.

Transitioning from being a prisoner of the past to a pioneer of the present is a profound journey of self-discovery and transformation. It involves letting go of past burdens, embracing the present moment, and fostering personal growth. Through introspection, forgiveness, acceptance, and self-compassion, we can break free from the shackles of our history and create a fulfilling, purpose-driven life. As we navigate this path, we not only transform our own lives but also inspire others to embark on their own journeys of growth and self-discovery. Remember, the power to change lies within you – all you need to do is take the first step.

CHAPTER EIGHT

Pleasing Everyone: A Futile Trap You Can Avoid

Have you ever found yourself bending over backward to make everyone happy, only to end up feeling exhausted, unappreciated, and lost in the process? If so, you're not alone. The desire to please everyone is a common trap, one that many of us fall into at some point in our lives. It's a journey fraught with stress, anxiety, and the perpetual fear of rejection. But here's the truth: pleasing everyone is not only impossible but also unnecessary. In this chapter, we will explore why this is a futile endeavor and how you can break free from its grip to lead a more authentic and fulfilling life.

The Illusion of Approval

Since childhood, we are ingrained with the desire to seek validation from others. As children, we look to our parents, teachers, and peers for validation. This need for acceptance is natural, a part of our social fabric. However, as we grow older, this quest for approval can become a burden, leading us to prioritize others' opinions over our own. The illusion of approval is like chasing a mirage; no matter how close you think you are; it always remains out of reach. The reality is that you can never satisfy everyone's expectations.

The Root of the Problem

At the heart of the need to please is a deep-seated fear of rejection and inadequacy. This fear drives us to seek constant validation, making us susceptible to others' expectations. We believe that by pleasing others, we can gain their acceptance and love. Yet, this belief is inherently flawed. Pleasing everyone often means compromising our values, desires, and authenticity. It leads to a fragmented identity, where our sense of self is dictated by others rather than by our own inner compass.

The Cost of People-Pleasing

The cost of trying to please everyone is high. It has the potential to deplete your energy reserves, diminish your self-esteem, and contribute to ongoing stress. You may find yourself in a cycle of over commitment, constantly saying "yes" to requests and demands, even when it means sacrificing your own needs and priorities. Over time, this behavior can result in burnout, resentment, and a sense of emptiness.

Emotional Toll

Emotionally, the pursuit of pleasing others can be devastating. When you base your worth on others' approval, you hand over your emotional well-being to external forces. This can lead to a rollercoaster of emotions, where your happiness is contingent on others‘ opinions and reactions. You might experience anxiety, guilt, and frustration when you can't meet everyone's expectations, leading to a vicious cycle of self-criticism and doubt.

Physical Consequences

The stress associated with people-pleasing can also evident physically. Chronic stress is linked to a host of health issues, including insomnia, headaches, digestive problems, and weakened immune function. Over time, the relentless pressure to satisfy others can take a toll on your physical health, leaving you depleted and vulnerable to illness.

Relationship Strain

Ironically, trying to please everyone can strain your relationships. When you constantly prioritize others' needs over your own, you may feel unappreciated and taken for granted. This can breed resentment and bitterness, undermining the very relationships you are trying to maintain. Furthermore, people may sense your inauthenticity, leading to superficial connections rather than deep, meaningful relationships.

The Path to Authenticity

Breaking free from the trap of pleasing everyone starts with a commitment to authenticity. Authenticity means being true to yourself, aligning your actions with your values, and embracing your unique identity. It involves setting boundaries, learning to say "no," and prioritizing your well-being.

The journey to authenticity and breaking free from the trap of pleasing everyone is a transformative process. By letting go of the need to please others, you can live a life that is true to your values, passions, and aspirations. Authenticity brings a sense of freedom, self-confidence, and fulfillment that is unattainable through external validation. Remember, you cannot please everyone, and that's perfectly okay. Embrace your authenticity, and you will discover a path to a more meaningful and joyful life.

CHAPTER NINE

INNER DIAMOND: LET IT SHINE

Have you ever paused to truly consider your worth? Not the kind that comes from external validation or societal accolades, but the intrinsic value that lies within your soul. Each of us is a masterpiece, sculpted by our experiences, dreams, and innermost desires. However, in the hustle and bustle of life, it's all too easy to forget our own significance. We often place others' needs and expectations above our own, diminishing our sense of self-worth in the process. But imagine if you could flip the script, prioritizing yourself first, and recognizing that by doing so, you can give more authentically and generously to the world.

Understanding self-worth starts with introspection. Take a moment to reflect on your life journey—each victory, each challenge, and each lesson learned.

As I delved deeper into self-reflection, I realized that understanding and valuing oneself is not an act of selfishness but a profound act of self-love. When you value yourself, you set a standard for how you should be treated. You teach others to respect your boundaries, to honor your feelings, and to appreciate your worth. It's about saying "yes" to yourself more often and understanding that your dreams and desires are valid and deserving of pursuit.

Imagine a world where you wake up each morning with a sense of purpose and a heart full of love for yourself. You greet the day not with dread or obligation, but with excitement for the opportunities it brings. You look in the mirror and see someone worthy of love, success, and happiness. This isn't a far-fetched dream; it's a reality that begins with the decision to prioritize yourself.

One of the most significant shifts happens when you start to say "no" without guilt. No to overextending yourself, no to toxic relationships, no to anything that drains your energy and dampens your spirit. It's about understanding that you are not responsible for fixing others or meeting their expectations at the expense of your well-being. By setting boundaries, you create space for growth, creativity, and joy in your life.

Consider the analogy of an airplane safety briefing: you're instructed to put on your oxygen mask before helping others. This is because you cannot assist anyone if you are not in a position of strength yourself. Similarly, in life, taking care of your needs first ensures that you are physically, emotionally, and mentally equipped to support those around you. It's not about being selfish; it's about being self-sufficient.

There will be moments of doubt and days when prioritizing yourself feels uncomfortable or even wrong. Society often glorifies self-sacrifice, especially for women, painting it as the ultimate act of love. But true love begins with loving oneself. It's about filling your cup so that you can pour from it generously. When you are fulfilled and happy, you become a beacon of positivity and strength for others. Your loved ones benefit from your vibrant energy and see a role model who values themselves.

During these transformative periods, you might face resistance, both internally and externally. Friends and family might not understand your new boundaries; they may even feel hurt or rejected. It's crucial to communicate openly and lovingly about your journey towards self-prioritization. Explain that by taking care of yourself, you are in a better place to nurture your relationships. Over time, they will see the positive changes and likely respect your choices.

Self-worth also involves celebrating your achievements, no matter how small they may seem. Often, we are quick to criticize ourselves and overlook our successes. Take time to acknowledge your accomplishments, whether it's completing a project at work, maintaining a healthy habit, or simply getting through a tough day. Every stride you take forward speaks volumes about your inner strength and unwavering resilience. Celebrate these moments, for they are the building blocks of your self-worth.

Moreover, embrace your imperfections. Society bombards us with images of perfection, creating unrealistic standards that can erode our self-esteem. Understand that imperfections are what make you unique and beautiful. They are the quirks and peculiarities that tell your story. Instead of striving for an unattainable ideal, focus on becoming the best version of yourself—one who is compassionate, loving, and true to your values.

In this journey towards self-worth, it's essential to surround yourself with positivity. Choose to be around people who uplift and inspire you, who see your value and encourage your growth. Distance yourself from negativity and those who belittle your worth. The way you perceive yourself is heavily influenced by your surroundings. Cultivate spaces—both physical and emotional—that nurture your well-being and allow you to thrive.

As you prioritize yourself, you'll find that your mental and emotional health improves. You'll experience less stress, better relationships, and a deeper sense of fulfillment. Your confidence will grow, and you'll become more comfortable taking risks and pursuing your dreams. This newfound strength and clarity will infuse every aspect of your life, from your career to your personal relationships.

It's also important to engage in practices that reinforce your self-worth. Meditation, journaling, and affirmations can be powerful tools in this process. Spend time each day reflecting on your values and goals, expressing gratitude for your strengths, and affirming your worthiness. These practices help to rewire your brain, creating new, positive thought patterns that support your self-esteem.

As you continue on this journey, remember that self-worth is not a destination but a continuous process. There will be ups and downs, moments of doubt, and times when you feel like you're not making progress. Allow yourself the patience to acknowledge that personal growth is a gradual process. Celebrate the small victories and be gentle with yourself during setbacks.

Your journey towards self-worth is also about giving yourself permission to be happy. Often, we tie our happiness to external factors—success, relationships, or material possessions. True happiness emanates from within ourselves. It's about finding joy in the present moment and appreciating the simple pleasures of life. It's about recognizing that you are deserving of happiness, not because of what you achieve, but simply because you are you.

Valuing your self-worth and prioritizing yourself is a powerful act of self-love. It's about understanding that you are inherently valuable and deserving of respect, love, and happiness. By putting yourself first, you create a strong foundation from which you can give more authentically to others. You become a source of inspiration and strength, a beacon of positivity in the lives of those around you. Embrace this journey with a spirit of openness and curiosity, and witness how your life unfolds into wonderfully unexpected paths of transformation.

CHAPTER TEN

GUILTY PLEASURES!

Have you ever found yourself indulging in something that brings you immense joy, only to be immediately followed by a pang of guilt? Perhaps it's the rich, decadent chocolate cake you can't resist, or those few hours lost in a captivating book when you "should" be working. These moments, these "guilty pleasures," are often seen as indulgences that we shouldn't allow ourselves, but let's take a moment to reframe this notion. What if these pleasures, when approached mindfully, are not sources of guilt, but rather gateways to a more fulfilled, confident, and authentic self?

First, let's understand what we mean by "guilty pleasures." They are activities or indulgences that bring us joy and satisfaction but are often accompanied by a sense of guilt or shame. Society, with its myriad of expectations and norms, has conditioned us to feel this way. We are taught to believe that true pleasure must be earned, and that any joy taken without sacrifice is somehow less valid. But is this really the case?

Imagine a life devoid of these little indulgences. It would be a life of pure functionality, where every action is driven by necessity rather than desire. In such a world, where would we find joy? How would we replenish our spirits? Guilty pleasures, when embraced without the accompanying guilt, can be powerful tools for self-care and personal growth. They provide a much-needed escape from the rigors of daily life and allow us to reconnect with our true selves.

Consider the simple pleasure of a quiet morning with a cup of your favorite coffee, savoring the aroma and the warmth as it spreads through your body. For some, this might feel like a stolen moment, a break from the constant grind. But what if, instead of feeling guilty, you acknowledged this moment as a necessary pause, a time to recharge and find balance? This change in viewpoint holds significant importance. It transforms a guilty pleasure into a conscious act of self-care.

The key lies in moderation and mindfulness. Guilty pleasures are not inherently harmful, but they can become detrimental if indulged excessively or at the expense of our responsibilities and relationships. It's about finding a balance where these pleasures enrich our lives without causing harm to ourselves or others. This balance is unique to each individual and requires introspection and honesty.

Take hobbies, for instance. Engaging in a hobby you love can be immensely fulfilling and a great way to practice self-growth. Whether it's painting, gardening, dancing, or even binge-watching your favorite series, these activities can offer a sense of accomplishment and joy. They allow us to explore our creativity, relieve stress, and even learn new skills. When we immerse ourselves in something we love, we tap into a deep well of potential and passion.

However, it's important to ensure that these pleasures are not deceptive or harmful to others. True pleasure should never come at the cost of someone else's well-being. This means being mindful of how our actions impact those around us. It means seeking joy in ways that are sustainable and considerate. For example, enjoying a piece of cake is a harmless indulgence, but if we indulge in it to the extent that it affects our health or becomes a source of deception in our lives, it crosses a line.

Self-growth and transformation often come from the most unexpected places. By embracing our guilty pleasures with mindfulness, we can use them as tools for self-discovery and confidence-building. Each indulgence, when chosen with care, can be a step towards becoming more comfortable in our own skin. It can be an affirmation of our right to experience joy, to prioritize our well-being, and to live authentically.

Let's take an example of someone who loves to dance but feels guilty about spending time on it because they think it's not productive. What if this person reframes their perspective and sees dancing as a form of exercise, a stress reliever, and a way to express themselves? By embracing this passion, they not only find joy but also improve their physical health, boost their mood, and gain confidence. This simple shift can transform a "guilty pleasure" into a powerful act of self-care and personal growth.

In conclusion, guilty pleasures are not something to be shunned or suppressed. Instead, they should be acknowledged and embraced as essential components of a balanced and fulfilling life. When approached with mindfulness and moderation, these pleasures can enhance our well-being, foster self-growth, and help us become more confident in our own skin. They remind us that joy is a vital part of the human experience and that we deserve to indulge in it without guilt.

So, the next time you find yourself savoring a piece of chocolate, losing yourself in a book, or dancing like no one is watching, do it with a full heart and a clear conscience. Embrace these moments of joy, for they are not just guilty pleasures—they are stepping stones on your journey to a happier, more authentic self.

I quote it here as “Can’t see the beauty around you? Maybe it’s time for the new lenses- Change your approach”

CHAPTER ELEVEN

Unleashing Positive Ripples

Have you ever felt the profound impact of a simple act of kindness? It's like a stone dropped into a still pond, sending ripples far beyond its initial point of contact. Kindness, at its essence, transcends mere action; it possesses the power to revolutionize lives, beginning from within ourselves.

Imagine a world where every action, every word spoken, and every thought harbored is infused with kindness. It's not just wishful thinking; it's a tangible reality waiting to be embraced. The essence of kindness lies not only in what we do but in how it reverberates through the interconnected web of humanity.

When you extend a helping hand to someone in need, whether through a smile, a supportive word, or a selfless deed, you set in motion a chain reaction. Your kindness may inspire that person to pay it forward, creating a domino effect of goodwill that transcends borders, cultures, and generations.

The essence of kindness transcends all boundaries of race, religion, and economic standing. It speaks a language understood by all—a language of empathy, compassion, and humanity. In a world often characterized by division and strife, kindness stands as a beacon of hope and healing.

But kindness is not solely about grand gestures or extravagant displays. It thrives in the little things—the everyday moments where we choose empathy over apathy, understanding over judgment, and love over indifference. It's about holding the door open for a stranger, lending a listening ear to a friend in distress, or offering a word of encouragement to someone facing challenges.

Research indicates that acts of kindness go beyond benefiting just the receiver; they also profoundly impact the giver. When you engage in acts of kindness, whether spontaneous or planned, your brain releases oxytocin and endorphins—chemicals associated with happiness and wellbeing. This "helper's high" not only boosts your mood but also reduces stress and strengthens your immune system.

Furthermore, kindness fosters a sense of connection and belonging. It builds bridges between individuals and communities, fostering trust and cooperation. In a society where isolation and loneliness are prevalent, kindness serves as a lifeline, forging bonds that sustain us through life's trials and tribulations.

The ripple effect of kindness extends beyond immediate interactions. It has the power to shape attitudes, shift paradigms, and create a more compassionate world. When communities come together in acts of collective kindness, they sow seeds of positivity that bear fruit in unexpected ways.

Moreover, kindness is a catalyst for personal growth and fulfillment. By cultivating a habit of kindness, you nurture qualities such as empathy, patience, and resilience. You learn to see the world through the eyes of others, gaining a deeper understanding of the shared human experience.

In essence, kindness is a gift that keeps on giving—a renewable resource that enriches both giver and receiver. It transcends individual actions to create a ripple effect of positivity that reverberates through society. As you embark on your journey of kindness, remember that no act is too small to make a difference.

The good you do will come back to you, not as a transaction but as a natural consequence of the kindness you spread. Embrace kindness as a way of life, and watch its ripple effect transform the world, one heart at a time. Some might think this contradicts the idea of prioritizing oneself, but it doesn't. Recognizing your own worth and practicing self-kindness are vital. Acts of kindness don't require you to sacrifice yourself; they simply involve offering emotional comfort or support to someone in need, whether you're aware of their struggle or not. The sense of satisfaction and peace that comes from these acts is profound. Begin by embracing kindness towards yourself, and let it radiate outward.

CHAPTER TWELVE

BLUEPRINT OF THE PRIORITY PYRAMID

The concept of a "priority pyramid" involves organizing tasks and values in a hierarchical structure, allowing for effective prioritization and focus. In the context of personal development, introspection, and transforming self-doubts into growth, this pyramid serves as a valuable tool to guide individuals towards self-improvement and actualization. By understanding and implementing a priority pyramid, one can systematically address and overcome self-doubts, fostering an environment conducive to personal growth.

The priority pyramid is built upon foundational elements that serve as the base for higher-level aspirations. In the context of introspection and personal growth, these foundational elements include:

1. **Self-Awareness:** The bedrock of the priority pyramid. Understanding oneself, recognizing strengths and weaknesses, and being aware of one's emotions and motivations is crucial for personal development. Self-awareness allows for honest introspection and forms the basis for addressing self-doubts.

2. **Core Values:** These are the guiding principles that shape one's actions and decisions. Identifying core values helps individuals align their behavior with their true self, providing a sense of purpose and direction.

3. **Basic Needs:** Physical and psychological needs must be met before higher-level aspirations can be pursued. These include safety, health, emotional stability, and a sense of belonging.

Levels of the Priority Pyramid

1. Self-Awareness and Acceptance

The first level involves developing self-awareness and acceptance which we have already covered in initial chapters. Introspection is a key component here, as it allows individuals to reflect on their experiences, emotions, and beliefs. By understanding the root causes of self-doubt, individuals can begin to accept themselves, recognizing that imperfections and challenges are part of the human experience.

- Introspection Practices: Journaling, meditation, and therapy are effective methods for introspection. These practices encourage self-reflection and help individuals gain clarity about their thoughts and feelings.

- Acceptance: Embracing one's flaws and limitations is essential for overcoming self-doubt. Acceptance doesn't mean contentment but rather acknowledging where one is starting from on the journey towards growth.

2. Identifying and Challenging Self-Doubts

The second level focuses on identifying specific self-doubts and challenging them. Self-doubts often stem from negative beliefs and past experiences. We have already covered methods unleashing from past experiences in previous chapters. The little depth of the techniques is in this subtopic. By pinpointing these doubts, individuals can begin to question their validity and replace them with more constructive thoughts.

- Cognitive Restructuring: This involves identifying negative thought patterns and reframing them in a positive light. For example, changing "I can't do this" to "I am capable of learning and improving."

- Evidence-Based Thinking: Encouraging individuals to seek evidence that contradicts their self-doubts. This might involve recalling past successes or gathering feedback from others to counteract negative beliefs.

3. Setting Realistic and Achievable Goals

With self-awareness and a clearer understanding of self-doubts, the next level involves setting realistic and achievable goals. The basic starts with, Goal-setting, provides a roadmap for personal growth and helps individuals focus their efforts on specific areas of improvement.

- SMART Goals: Goals should be defined clearly and specifically, measurable to track progress, achievable and realistic, relevant to your overall objectives, and set within a specific timeframe.

- Incremental Progress: Breaking larger goals into smaller, manageable steps allows for steady progress and builds confidence over time.

4. Developing Skills and Competencies

The fourth level emphasizes skill development and competency building. Overcoming self-doubts often requires acquiring new skills or improving existing ones. This level focuses on practical actions to enhance one's abilities.

- Continuous Learning: Engaging in lifelong learning through courses, workshops, reading, and other educational opportunities.

- Skill Practice: Regular practice and application of new skills to build competence and confidence.

5. Building a Support System

A strong network of support is essential for personal development. This level involves surrounding oneself with supportive individuals who provide encouragement, feedback, and accountability.

- Mentorship and Coaching: Seeking guidance from mentors or coaches who can offer insights and support based on their experience and expertise.

- Peer Support: Engaging with like-minded individuals or groups who share similar goals and challenges, fostering a sense of community and mutual encouragement.

6. Reflecting and Adjusting

The final level of the priority pyramid involves ongoing reflection and adjustment. Personal growth is a continuous process, and regular reflection allows individuals to assess their progress, celebrate achievements, and make necessary adjustments to their goals and strategies.

- Regular Check-Ins: Scheduling regular times for self-reflection to evaluate progress and make adjustments as needed.

- Adaptability: Being open to change and willing to modify goals and strategies based on new insights and experiences.

The blueprint of the pyramid has been shared but human always crave for more. I will share my practical experiences and we will dive deeper into the ocean of introspection. Are you ready my scuba buddies?

CHAPTER THIRTEEN

Hear the Voices Around You: Unlock Potential

In the bustling symphony of life, where the cacophony of voices often drowns out the whispers of wisdom, the art of listening is a powerful tool that can unlock untold potential. This chapter delves into the profound impact of truly hearing the voices around you, emphasizing that listening is not just about processing sounds, but about understanding perspectives, gathering insights, and fostering growth. By becoming an effective listener, we can transcend the limitations of our own understanding, avoid the pitfalls of gossip, and act thoughtfully and intentionally on the information we receive. Above all, this approach helps us to introspect and grow both personally and professionally.

The Power of Listening

Listening is more than a passive act; it is an active engagement with the world around us. It involves paying attention, interpreting, and responding to the messages we receive from others. When we listen effectively, we open ourselves to a wealth of perspectives and experiences that can enrich our own understanding and inform our decisions.

Understanding Perspectives

Every individual we encounter carries a unique set of experiences, beliefs, and knowledge. By listening to them, we gain access to these diverse perspectives, which can broaden our own views and challenge our preconceived notions. This expanded understanding is invaluable in navigating the complexities of both personal and professional life.

Consider a scenario in the workplace where a project faces challenges. By listening to the team members' diverse viewpoints, a leader can identify the root causes of the problems, uncover creative solutions, and foster a collaborative environment. This not only leads to better outcomes for the project but also builds a stronger, more organized team.

Overcoming Limited Understanding

Our understanding of any given situation is inherently limited by our personal experiences and biases. When we fail to listen to others, we take risk making decisions based on incomplete or skewed information. Effective listening helps us to fill these gaps and make more informed choices.

Avoiding Gossip and Acting on Facts

Listening effectively also means distinguishing between constructive information and harmful gossip. Gossip can erode trust, create divisions, and undermine morale. By focusing on facts and verified information, we can make decisions that are fair, informed, and respectful of others.

The Dangers of Gossip

Gossip often thrives on speculation and negativity, spreading misinformation and creating a toxic environment. It can distort our perception of reality and lead us to make judgments based on incomplete or false information. To avoid these pitfalls, it is crucial to verify the information we hear and refrain from passing on unverified or harmful rumors.

Hearing, Not Treating as Directive

While listening to others is essential, it is equally important to remember that not all information should be treated as a directive. We must learn to weigh the perspectives we receive, integrate them with our own understanding, and make decisions that align with our values and goals.

Critical Evaluation

Critical evaluation involves assessing the reliability and relevance of the information we receive. This means considering the source, context, and potential biases of the information, and determining how it fits with our own knowledge and experiences. By engaging in this practice, we empower ourselves to make decisions that are well-informed and balanced.

Balancing Perspectives

Balancing perspectives requires us to integrate the insights we gain from others with our own judgment. This process involves reflecting on the information we receive, considering its implications, and deciding how best to act on it. It also means recognizing that we are ultimately responsible for our own decisions and actions.

To become more effective listeners, we can adopt practical strategies such as practicing active listening, avoiding interruptions, staying open-minded, verifying information, reflecting on feedback, and encouraging open communication. By doing so, we can unlock the potential that lies within the voices around us and create a more informed, connected, and empowered life.

Hear Voices of within

Have you ever paused to truly hear the voices within you? These gentle whispers, often dismissed amidst the chaos of daily life, hold the essence of your intuition. Intuition is that quiet, persistent feeling guiding you towards the best decisions, illuminating the path of growth. It's like an inner compass, always pointing you in the right direction, even when logic and reason seem to argue otherwise. Trusting these inner voices can be incredibly effective, leading to choices that resonate with your true self and fostering personal and professional growth. Women, in particular, are often more attuned to their intuitive side. Perhaps it's a deeper connection to emotions, a heightened sense of empathy, or a nurturing spirit that makes women more receptive to these subtle cues. Yet, despite this innate gift, many humans, irrespective of gender, often reject their intuition, drowning it in self-doubt. We question our inner wisdom, allowing fear and uncertainty to cloud our judgment. This self-doubt can stem from societal pressures, past experiences, or a lack of confidence in our own abilities. But when we silence these doubts and listen, truly listen, to our inner voices, we discover a wellspring of guidance and clarity. By embracing our intuition, we tap into a profound source of wisdom that can lead us to more fulfilling and authentic lives. So next time you face a decision, take a moment to quiet your mind, breathe deeply, and hear the voices within you. Trust that inner whisper. It knows you better than anyone else, and it will always steer you towards what is best for you. In this delicate dance between mind and heart, let intuition be your most trusted partner, leading you towards growth and the realization of your true potential.

Hearing the voices around us and within us is a powerful tool for unlocking potential. By listening effectively, we can gather diverse perspectives, overcome our limited understanding, and make more informed decisions and intuitive decisions. Avoiding gossip and focusing on facts helps us maintain integrity and build trust. While it is important to hear and consider the perspectives of others, we must also remember to critically evaluate the information we receive and integrate it with our own judgment.

In the era of podcasts, we have vast opportunities to clear the thought process and have positive productive mindsets. In the symphony of life, every voice has its own unique melody. By listening to these melodies, we can create a richer, more harmonious existence. So, let us tune in, hear the voices around us and within us, and unlock the limitless potential that lies within.

CHAPTER FOURTEEN

Talk Your Way to the Top: Speak and Be Heard

In the journey of personal and professional growth, communication is a critical skill that often determines our success. Now that we have an insight on hear the voices around to unlock our true potential, the communication is always a two-way process, Thus, lets delve into the other part of the process, "Talk Your Way to the Top: Speak and Be Heard" explores the profound impact of being vocal and assertive in expressing our perspectives, sharing our hardships, and celebrating our achievements. This chapter delves into the importance of overcoming self-doubt and transforming it into growth through the power of speech.

The Power of Being Vocal

Being vocal is more than just speaking; it is about effectively conveying our thoughts, feelings, and experiences. It involves articulating our ideas clearly and confidently, ensuring that our message resonates with the audience. By being vocal, we assert our presence, validate our experiences, and influence others positively.

The Impact of Effective Communication

Effective communication bridges gaps, resolves misunderstandings, and fosters collaboration. When we speak up, we:

1. **Build Connections:** Sharing our stories helps others relate to us, fostering empathy and building stronger relationships.

2. **Influence Decisions:** Our words can shape opinions, guide actions, and drive change.

3. **Assert Our Needs:** Communicating our needs and boundaries ensures they are respected, leading to more fulfilling interactions.

4. **Enhance Visibility:** Being vocal makes us more visible, increasing our opportunities for growth and recognition.

Overcoming Self-Doubt

Self-doubt is a common barrier to effective communication. It stems from fear of judgment, rejection, or failure. Overcoming self-doubt is crucial to becoming a confident speaker. Acknowledging your worth, constructive feedback, embrace mistakes, active listening, sharing your perspective clearly and concisely, etc. are some strategies to transform self-doubt into growth.

Talking your way to the top is not about dominating conversations or being the loudest voice in the room. It's about communicating effectively, authentically, and with integrity. By being vocal, you ensure your perspective is heard, your hardships are understood, and your achievements are recognized. This process not only enhances your personal and professional growth but also inspires and influences those around you.

Embrace the power of your voice. Speak confidently, listen actively, and communicate with purpose. In doing so, you will transform self-doubt into growth, build meaningful connections, and pave the way for your success. Remember, your voice matters. Use it wisely and boldly to talk your way to the top.

CHAPTER FIFTEEN

Out of The Box Infused with Integrity

In a world that often values quick results and immediate gratification, the concept of thinking "out of the box" infused with integrity stands as a beacon of hope and sustainability. This chapter explores the profound impact of combining innovative thinking with a steadfast commitment to integrity, showcasing how this powerful synergy can lead to positive and effective alternatives in our actions and behaviors. Whether in personal growth, professional development, or societal contributions, embracing creativity with integrity can transform challenges into opportunities and conflicts into collaborations.

Understanding the Box

The "box" symbolizes the conventional ways of thinking and acting. It represents the familiar routines, the standard procedures, and the societal norms that dictate much of our behavior. While staying within the box can provide comfort and predictability, it often limits our potential and stifles innovation. Stepping outside this box involves challenging assumptions, questioning the status quo, and daring to explore new possibilities.

However, stepping out of the box without a moral compass can lead to reckless decisions and unethical practices. Integrity becomes paramount in this scenario. Integrity embodies the essence of honesty and steadfast adherence to moral principles. It signifies unwavering commitment to truthfulness and ethical values in all actions and decisions. It is the foundation that ensures our innovative ideas are not only creative but also ethical and sustainable.

The Intersection of Creativity and Integrity

The intersection of creativity and integrity is a powerful space. Creativity without integrity can lead to exploitation, deceit, and short-term gains at the expense of long-term consequences. On the other hand, integrity without creativity can result in rigidity, resistance to change, and missed opportunities. Combining the two creates a balanced approach that fosters innovation while maintaining ethical standards.

Case Study: Apple Inc.

Apple Inc. is a prime example of a company that has successfully merged creativity with integrity. Under the leadership of Steve Jobs, Apple was known for its out-of-the-box thinking, revolutionizing the tech industry with products like the iPhone, iPad, and MacBook. However, alongside this innovation, Apple maintained a strong commitment to integrity, focusing on customer privacy, environmental sustainability, and ethical labor practices. This combination of creativity and integrity has not only led to groundbreaking products but also built a loyal customer base and a respected brand.

Positive and Effective Alternatives

For every action and behavior, there is always a positive and effective alternative that aligns with integrity. This section will explore several scenarios where thinking out of the box, infused with integrity, can lead to better outcomes.

Conflict arises inevitably in the course of human interaction. Whether it's a disagreement with a colleague, a misunderstanding with a friend, or a family dispute, conflicts can escalate quickly if not handled properly. The conventional approach to conflict resolution often involves compromise or confrontation. However, by thinking out of the box and infusing integrity into the process, we can find more positive and effective alternatives.

In the workplace, the pressure to perform and achieve can sometimes lead to unethical behavior, such as cutting corners or undermining colleagues. Traditional career advancement strategies often focus on aggressive competition and self-promotion. However, by thinking out of the box and integrating integrity into our professional development, we can find alternatives that are not only ethical but also more fulfilling and sustainable.

Personal growth often involves stepping out of our comfort zones and challenging ourselves to achieve new heights. The conventional approach might focus on setting ambitious goals and pushing ourselves relentlessly to achieve them. However, without integrity, this can lead to burnout, stress, and ethical compromises. By thinking out of the box and infusing integrity into our personal growth journey, we can find healthier and more effective alternatives.

As members of society, we have the opportunity to contribute to the greater good. Traditional approaches to societal contributions often involve charity and philanthropy. While these are valuable, thinking out of the box and infusing integrity into our societal contributions can lead to more impactful and sustainable outcomes.

The Role of Mindset

Adopting an out-of-the-box mindset infused with integrity requires a shift in how we perceive challenges and opportunities. It involves cultivating a mindset that is open, curious, and committed to ethical principles. Here are some key aspects of this mindset:

Curiosity and Openness

Curiosity drives us to explore new ideas and perspectives. By remaining open to different viewpoints and experiences, we can discover innovative solutions that we might otherwise overlook. This openness also allows us to embrace diversity and inclusivity, recognizing the value that different backgrounds and perspectives bring to the table.

Resilience and Adaptability

Stepping out of the box often involves facing uncertainty and setbacks. Resilience and adaptability are crucial in navigating these challenges. By maintaining a positive attitude and being willing to adjust our approach, we can overcome obstacles and continue moving forward with integrity.

Commitment to Values

A strong commitment to our values serves as a guiding light in our journey of innovation and integrity. By regularly reflecting on our values and ensuring that our actions align with them, we can stay true to ourselves and make decisions that are both creative and ethical.

Courage and Authenticity

It takes courage to step out of the box and challenge the status quo. Embracing authenticity, being true to ourselves, and standing up for what we believe in, even in the face of opposition, are essential components of this mindset. Authenticity also fosters trust and respect, both within ourselves and in our interactions with others.

Thinking out of the box infused with integrity is not just a strategy for success; it is a philosophy that can transform our lives, our relationships, and our contributions to society. By embracing creativity with a commitment to ethical principles, we can navigate challenges with resilience, find innovative solutions to complex problems, and make a positive impact on the world around us.

As we move forward, let us remember that for every action and behavior, there is always a positive and effective alternative that aligns with integrity. By cultivating an out-of-the-box mindset, grounded in our core values, we can create a future that is not only innovative but also just, sustainable, and fulfilling for all.

CHAPTER SIXTEEN

VISUALIZE TO REALIZE: PAINT YOUR MIND'S CANVAS

Have you ever sat quietly and let your mind wander, allowing your imagination to soar beyond the limits of reality? If not, then it's time to embark on this transformative journey of visualization. Picture this: your mind is a vast canvas, waiting for you to paint your dreams, aspirations, and the very essence of who you wish to become. The power of visualization is not just a mystical concept; it's a practical tool that can turn your self-doubt into self-growth, leading you toward a life of fulfillment and purpose.

Visualization is a profound method that allows you to create mental images of your desired outcomes. It's more than daydreaming; it's about harnessing the power of your mind to envision the life you want and, in doing so, making it a reality. When we visualize, we are not just imagining; we are engaging in a process that can rewire our brain, influence our emotions, and guide our actions. Let's delve into how this remarkable practice can help you transform self-doubt into self-growth through introspection.

Have you ever paused to consider when someone poses the question, "Imagine yourself bald—how would you appear?" or "Imagine that person with vampire teeth," you instantly create a mental picture and often laugh? Many of us are naturally skilled at imagining things. That's exactly what visualization is about. Just as we can quickly picture funny or unusual scenarios, we can also imagine ourselves achieving the success we desire. Visualization is a powerful tool for fostering a positive outlook and transforming self-doubt into self-growth. What we need are the right techniques and consistent practice.

Imagine you are standing at the edge of a cliff, looking down at a vast, empty canvas stretching out beneath you. This canvas represents your life, with every brushstroke symbolizing your thoughts, beliefs, and actions. Now, take a moment to reflect on the self-doubt that has been holding you back. These doubts are like dark clouds looming over your canvas, preventing you from seeing the vibrant colors of your potential. But what if you could use visualization to dissipate these clouds and reveal the true masterpiece beneath?

Now, let's bring visualization into the picture. Close your eyes and imagine yourself in a quiet, serene place—a place where you feel safe and at peace. This could be a beautiful beach, a tranquil forest, or a cozy room filled with warm light. As you settle into this space, visualize yourself standing in front of a mirror. This mirror is special; it doesn't just reflect your physical appearance but also the thoughts and beliefs that reside within you.

Take a deep breath and look into the mirror. What do you see? You might see the self-doubt as shadows or distortions in the reflection. Acknowledge these shadows without judgment. They are integral to your being, yet they do not encompass your entirety. As you continue to gaze into the mirror, imagine a gentle light emanating from within you, growing stronger with each breath. This light symbolizes the reservoir of strength and untapped potential within you. Let it fill the reflection, gradually pushing away the shadows of self-doubt.

In this moment, you are witnessing the power of visualization. By creating a mental image of yourself filled with light and strength, you are beginning to change the narrative you tell yourself. This practice is not about denying the existence of self-doubt but about recognizing your capacity to transform it. Visualization helps you see beyond the limitations imposed by your mind and opens up a realm of possibilities.

This process of visualization does more than just create a temporary sense of confidence. It actively rewires your brain. Neuroscientists have discovered that when we visualize an action, we stimulate the same brain regions as when we actually perform that action. This means that through repeated visualization, you are training your brain to respond differently to situations that typically trigger self-doubt. You are creating new neural pathways that support confidence and self-belief.

Let's take this a step further and incorporate goal setting into your visualization practice. Goal setting is an integral part of personal growth, and when combined with visualization, it becomes even more potent. Start by identifying a goal you want to achieve. From conquering marathons to crafting your entrepreneurial journey, dreams come in all shapes and sizes. Once you have your goal, break it down into smaller, manageable steps.

Now, visualize each step in vivid detail. See yourself completing each task, overcoming obstacles, and moving closer to your goal. For instance, if your goal is to run a marathon, visualize yourself putting on your running shoes, feeling the ground beneath your feet as you train, and crossing the finish line with a sense of accomplishment. Feel the exhilaration, the sweat on your skin, and the cheers from the crowd. The more sensory details you include, the more real it becomes in your mind.

This practice does more than just keep you motivated; it also helps you anticipate challenges and mentally prepare for them. By visualizing both the journey and the outcome, you are equipping yourself with the resilience needed to overcome setbacks. When self-doubt creeps in, reminding you of past failures or whispering fears of future ones, you can return to your visualizations. These mental images act as anchors, grounding you in your potential and reminding you of your progress.

Another powerful aspect of visualization is its ability to shift your focus from what you fear to what you desire. Self-doubt often stems from a fear of the unknown or a fixation on negative outcomes. By consciously directing your mind towards positive visions, you are training yourself to focus on possibilities rather than limitations. This shift in perspective is crucial for fostering a growth mindset.

Embracing a growth mindset means acknowledging that skills and intelligence can evolve through persistent effort and determination, in stark contrast to a fixed mindset that views abilities as rigid and immutable. Visualization nurtures a growth mindset by reinforcing the idea that you have the power to shape your future. It inspires you to view challenges as chances for personal evolution rather than challenges to your self-value.

To make visualization a consistent part of your life, create a daily routine around it. Dedicate a few moments daily to hone your craft. Find a quiet space where you won't be disturbed, close your eyes, and let your imagination take over. Begin with a few deep breaths to center yourself, then start visualizing your goals and the person you aspire to be. As you do this, pay attention to the emotions that arise. Allow yourself to feel the joy, excitement, and pride of achieving your dreams.

Visualization can also be enhanced by incorporating other senses. If you're visualizing a beach, imagine the sound of the waves, the smell of the salty air, and the warmth of the sun on your skin. Engaging multiple senses makes the experience more immersive and effective. Additionally, you can use tools like vision boards, where you create a collage of images and words that represent your goals and dreams. Place your vision board somewhere you'll see it daily as a constant reminder of what you're working towards.

Remember, visualization is not a magical solution that will instantly erase self-doubt or guarantee success. It is a practice that requires consistency and patience. There will be days when your mind resists, when the shadows of doubt seem particularly stubborn. On those days, be gentle with yourself. Acknowledge the difficulty and remind yourself that growth is a journey, not a destination.

As you continue this practice, you'll start to notice subtle shifts in your mindset and behavior. You'll find yourself approaching challenges with more confidence, taking risks you previously avoided, and celebrating small victories along the way. The transformation from self-doubt to self-growth is not always dramatic; it often happens in small, almost imperceptible steps. But each step is significant, bringing you closer to the person you are meant to be.

In this journey, introspection remains a constant companion. Regularly take time to reflect on your progress. Journaling can be a helpful tool for this. Write down your thoughts, feelings, and observations about your visualization practice and its impact on your life. Embrace every achievement, big or small, and grow stronger with every challenge you face. Use these reflections to refine your visualizations, making them more aligned with your evolving goals and aspirations.

Ultimately, the practice of visualization is about reclaiming your agency. It's about recognizing that you have the power to shape your thoughts, influence your emotions, and direct your actions. By painting your mind's canvas with images of possibility and success, you are creating a blueprint for your future. You are not just a passive observer of your life but an active participant in its creation.

So, take a deep breath and look at your canvas once more. See the vibrant colors of your dreams, the bold strokes of your aspirations, and the intricate details of your journey. Know that with each brushstroke, you are transforming self-doubt into self-growth. You are painting a masterpiece that reflects the true essence of who you are and who you are becoming. And as you continue to visualize, to introspect, and to grow, remember that this canvas is yours to create, every day, with every thought, and with every breath.

In this chapter, we have explored the profound impact of visualization on personal growth. By harnessing the power of your mind, you can turn your dreams into reality and transform self-doubt into self-belief. This practice, combined with introspection and goal setting, provides a powerful framework for personal development. As you continue on this journey, embrace the process, trust in your potential, and keep painting your mind's canvas with the colors of possibility. Your masterpiece is waiting to be realized.

CHAPTER SEVENTEEN

The Silver Lining: The Art of Bouncing Back

Life's journey winds through peaks and valleys, weaving through unforeseen obstacles and moments of triumph, where resilience triumphs over adversity's grasp. However, the ability to bounce back, to find the silver lining in every cloud, is what sets resilient individuals apart. This chapter delves into the essentials of optimism and positive mindsets, exploring techniques to shift from a negative outlook to a resilient and empowered approach to life.

The Power of Optimism

Optimism is more than just a cheerful disposition; it is a powerful mindset that can transform the way we experience and respond to life's challenges. At its core, optimism is the belief that good things will happen and that setbacks are temporary and manageable. This positive outlook is not about denying reality or ignoring problems; rather, it is about facing difficulties with a hopeful and proactive attitude.

Research has shown that optimism is linked to numerous benefits, including better physical health, increased longevity, and greater overall well-being. Optimists tend to have lower stress levels, more robust immune systems, and a greater capacity to cope with adversity. This is because they view challenges as opportunities for growth and learning, rather than insurmountable obstacles.

Imagine you are walking through a dense forest, and suddenly, a storm breaks out. An optimist sees the storm as a temporary disruption, a part of the journey, and believes that they will eventually find shelter and sunshine. They focus on finding solutions and maintaining hope. A pessimist, on the other hand, may feel overwhelmed by the storm, believing it to be an endless downpour, and struggle to see a way out. The key difference lies in their perspective.

Cultivating a Positive Mindset

Cultivating a positive mindset involves more than just adopting a "glass-half-full" attitude. It requires a conscious effort to reframe negative thoughts and develop habits that support resilience. Foster a positive mindset and bounce back from setbacks through practicing gratitude, reframing negative thoughts, setting realistic goals, surrounding yourself with positivity and actively participating mindfulness activities, etc.

Techniques to Bounce Back

Bouncing back from a negative mindset involves practical strategies that can help you regain your footing and move forward with renewed strength. Here are some techniques to help you recover from setbacks and build a resilient mindset:

1. **Acknowledge Your Feelings:** It's important to recognize and accept your emotions, even the negative ones. Suppressing or denying your feelings can lead to increased stress and emotional turmoil. Allow yourself to feel and process your emotions before moving forward.

2. **Learn from Setbacks:** Every setback carries a lesson. Take a moment to introspect on setbacks, uncovering the lessons they hold for personal growth. This mindset transforms failures into valuable opportunities for growth and improvement.

3. **Focus on What You Can Control:** In difficult situations, it's easy to feel overwhelmed by factors beyond your control. Redirect your attention to areas where you hold influence, and initiate proactive measures to effect positive change. This approach empowers you to take meaningful action and regain a sense of agency.

4. **Set New Goals:** After a setback, reevaluate your goals and set new ones that align with your current circumstances. This forward-thinking approach

helps you stay focused on the future and maintain momentum.

5. **Seek Support:** Don't hesitate to reach out to friends, family, or a mentor for support and guidance. Sharing your experiences and gaining perspective from others can provide comfort and clarity.

6. **Embrace self-compassion:** Extend to yourself the kindness and understanding you readily give to others, particularly in challenging moments. Remember that setbacks are a natural part of the human experience, and you are not alone.

7. **Celebrate Tiniest Wins:** Embrace Every Step: Acknowledge and celebrate each stride forward, regardless of its size. Every stride forward, regardless of its size, propels you closer to achieving your aspirations. Celebrating these wins reinforces a positive mindset and builds confidence.

Bouncing back from setbacks is a journey, not a destination. Achieving personal growth demands continual dedication, introspection, and a steadfast commitment to progress. As you navigate this journey, remember that resilience is not about never falling but about rising each time you do.

Consider the analogy of a seed blossoming into a towering tree. In mythology, the phoenix is a symbol of renewal and rebirth. It burns and crumbles, only to rise again, stronger and more vibrant. This powerful image reminds us that our struggles and setbacks do not define us. Instead, they provide the opportunity for transformation and growth.

As you continue to cultivate optimism and resilience, you will find that the setbacks you face become stepping stones rather than stumbling blocks. You will develop a deeper sense of self-efficacy and confidence in your ability to overcome challenges. This newfound strength will enable you to approach life with greater courage and enthusiasm.

The art of bouncing back lies in our ability to find the silver lining in every cloud, to see challenges as opportunities for growth, and to cultivate a mindset of resilience and optimism. By embracing the techniques and practices outlined in this chapter, you can transform setbacks into stepping stones and build a life filled with purpose, joy, and fulfillment. Remember, every storm eventually passes, and with each one, you have the chance to rise stronger and more resilient than before. Your journey is unique, and your capacity to bounce back is limitless. Embrace the silver lining and let it guide you towards a brighter, more empowered future.

CHAPTER EIGHTEEN

Dream Big, Live Small!

In a world often defined by excess and accumulation, the concept of living small while dreaming big may initially seem counterintuitive. Yet, beneath the surface lies a profound truth: embracing minimalism can be a powerful catalyst for personal growth, transforming self-doubt into boundless potential. Let us embark on a journey into the heart of minimalism and discover how it can pave the way to a life filled with purpose, clarity, and fulfillment.

Understanding Minimalism

At its core, minimalism is not merely about owning fewer possessions or living in a tiny space. It is a deliberate choice to simplify one's life by focusing on what truly matters. It encourages us to strip away the unnecessary distractions and noise that often cloud our thoughts and goals. By decluttering our physical environment, we create room for mental clarity and emotional well-being. This clarity forms the foundation upon which we can build our dreams.

Dreaming Big: The Power of Vision

Dreams are the seeds of our aspirations, the fuel that propels us forward in life. They inspire us to reach beyond our current circumstances and envision a future filled with possibility. Whether it's starting a business, writing a novel, traveling the world, or making a significant impact in our community, our dreams define the path we choose to tread.

The Paradox of Minimalism and Ambition

Contrary to popular belief, minimalism and ambition are not mutually exclusive. Indeed, they enhance each other in meaningful ways. By simplifying our lives and shedding the unnecessary, we free up resources—both physical and mental—that can be directed towards nurturing our dreams. When we eliminate distractions and focus on what truly matters, we become more intentional and disciplined in pursuing our ambitions.

From Self-Doubt to Self-Growth: The Minimalist Mindset

Self-doubt is a common adversary on the journey towards personal growth. It whispers tales of inadequacy, fear of failure, and the temptation to conform to societal expectations. However, minimalism offers a refreshing perspective. By consciously choosing to live with less, we challenge the notion that our worth is tied to material possessions or external validation. Instead, we cultivate an inner resilience built on authenticity and self-awareness.

Embracing Simplicity: Finding Fulfillment Beyond Materialism

In a consumer-driven culture, we are often conditioned to equate success with the accumulation of wealth and possessions. Minimalism challenges this paradigm by emphasizing experiences over things, quality over quantity, and intrinsic values over external validation. By prioritizing relationships, personal growth, and meaningful experiences, we discover a deeper sense of fulfillment that transcends materialism.

Practical Steps Towards Minimalist Living

Transitioning to a minimalist lifestyle is a gradual process that requires intentional choices and mindful practices. Start by evaluating your current possessions and identifying items that truly add value to your life. Simplify your living space by decluttering and organizing with purpose. Cultivate mindful consumption habits by resisting the urge to impulse buy and focusing on purchasing items that align with your values and long-term goals.

Mindful Consumption: Making Conscious Choices

Minimalism extends beyond physical possessions to encompass all aspects of our lives, including our time, energy, and attention. Practice mindfulness in your daily routines by prioritizing activities that nurture your well-being and align with your aspirations. Set boundaries to protect your time and energy from distractions that hinder your progress towards your dreams.

The Transformative Power of Less: Insights from Minimalist Practitioners

Throughout history, many influential figures have embraced minimalism as a pathway to clarity, creativity, and success. From artists and writers who thrived in minimalist environments to entrepreneurs who streamlined their businesses for greater efficiency, their stories illustrate the transformative power of less. By focusing on what truly matters and eliminating distractions, they unlocked new levels of productivity and innovation.

Living Small, Dreaming Big: A Personal Journey

Imagine waking up each morning to a living space that is serene and uncluttered, where every item serves a purpose and brings joy. Visualize a life where your time and energy are invested in pursuits that ignite your passion and align with your values. This is the essence of living small while dreaming big—a harmonious balance between simplicity and ambition.

Achieving Balance: Integrating Minimalism into Your Everyday Life

As you embark on your own journey of minimalist living, remember that it is not about deprivation or sacrifice but about conscious choice and intentional living. Embrace the freedom that comes from letting go of excess and embracing the essentials. Nurture your dreams with clarity and purpose, knowing that every step towards simplicity is a step towards self-discovery and growth.

Thepath to personal growth begins with a mindset shift—an acknowledgment that true fulfillment comes from within, not from external possessions or achievements. By embracing minimalism, we create space for introspection, creativity, and meaningful connections. We empower ourselves to break free from self-doubt and embrace the limitless potential that resides within us. So, dare to dream big and live small. Embrace the simplicity that leads to clarity, and let your aspirations guide you towards a life of purpose and fulfillment.

CHAPTER NINETEEN

The Power of Now: Procrastination End, Growth Start

Procrastination is a silent thief that robs us of our most precious resource: time. It is the habit of delaying tasks, often replacing them with more pleasurable activities, and it is one of the biggest barriers to personal and professional growth. The power of "now" lies in its ability to dismantle procrastination and unlock our potential. Understanding the roots of procrastination and employing techniques to overcome it can transform our lives, turning stagnation into growth and missed opportunities into accomplishments.

Procrastination frequently originates from a complex interplay of psychological elements, such as the dread of failing, striving for perfection, insufficient motivation, and a sense of being overwhelmed. It creates a vicious cycle where the more we delay, the more anxious and stressed we become, which in turn leads to further procrastination. This habit can prevent us from achieving our goals, hinder our personal development, and affect our overall well-being.

Diagnosing Procrastination

Embarking on the journey to conquer procrastination begins with acknowledging its presence. Procrastination can manifest in subtle ways, such as spending excessive time on social media, engaging in unproductive tasks, or making endless to-do lists without taking action. Acknowledging that we are procrastinating and understanding the reasons behind it is crucial for addressing the issue.

The Cost of Procrastination

The cost of procrastination is high. It can lead to missed deadlines, poor performance, and diminished self-esteem. When we procrastinate, we not only delay our tasks but also our progress and growth. The guilt and stress associated with procrastination can negatively impact our mental health, leading to a lack of motivation and increased anxiety. The longer we put off important tasks, the more daunting they become, creating a cycle of avoidance and frustration.

Skills to Vanquish Procrastination

1. **Set Clear Goals:** Clear, achievable goals provide direction and purpose. Take complex tasks, break them into smaller steps, and assign deadlines to each step for efficient completion. This approach reduces the feeling of being overwhelmed and makes tasks more approachable.

2. **Prioritize Tasks:** Use techniques such as the Eisenhower Matrix to prioritize tasks based on their urgency and importance. Focus on high-priority tasks that contribute to your long-term goals. Completing important tasks first can boost your motivation and productivity.

3. **Create a Structured Schedule:** Develop a daily or weekly schedule that allocates specific time slots for each task. Stick to this schedule to build a routine and maintain discipline. Having a structured plan reduces the temptation to procrastinate.

4. **Use Time Management Techniques:** Techniques like the Pomodoro Technique, where you work for 25 minutes and take a 5-minute break, can enhance focus and productivity. These intervals of focused work followed by short breaks can help maintain momentum and reduce burnout.

5. **Eliminate Distractions:** Identify and eliminate distractions in your environment. This could entail disabling notifications, establishing a designated workspace, or defining limits in interactions with others. A distraction-free environment allows for deeper focus and concentration.

6. **Mindfulness Drill:** Embracing mindfulness means immersing yourself fully in the present, fostering focus, reducing anxiety, and bolstering commitment through practices like meditation and deep breathing.

7. **Recompense Yourself:** Create a reward system for completing tasks. Rewarding yourself for meeting deadlines or achieving milestones can boost motivation and make the process more enjoyable. Rewards come in various forms, whether it's a moment to unwind, savoring a beloved treat, or indulging in a favorite pastime.

8. **Hunt for Accountability:** Share your aspirations and timelines with a trusted friend, family member, or mentor who can support and keep you accountable. Regular check-ins and progress updates can provide external motivation and support, making it harder to procrastinate.

9. **Visualize Success:** Visualization involves imagining the successful completion of your tasks and the positive outcomes that follow. Visualizing success can increase motivation, boost confidence, and reduce the fear of failure that often fuels procrastination.

10. **Address Underlying Issues:** Sometimes, procrastination is a symptom of deeper issues such as fear, self-doubt, or perfectionism. Addressing these underlying issues through self-reflection, counseling, or coaching can help break the cycle of procrastination.

The Power of Now

Embracing the power of now means taking immediate action and focusing on the present moment. When we prioritize the present, we shift our mindset from one of delay to one of action. This shift can have profound effects on our productivity, personal growth, and overall satisfaction.

Living in the present moment allows us to fully engage with our tasks, reduce stress, and enhance our overall well-being. It enables us to take advantage of opportunities as they arise and make the most of our time. By focusing on the now, we can overcome the paralysis of procrastination and build momentum towards our goals.

Transforming Procrastination into Growth

Overcoming procrastination demands a voyage of patience, unwavering persistence, and embracing oneself with gentle compassion. It involves changing deeply ingrained habits and beliefs about our abilities and worth. By employing the techniques mentioned above, we can transform procrastination from a barrier into a stepping stone for growth.

Each time we choose to act rather than delay, we build confidence in our abilities. Completing tasks and achieving goals reinforces a positive cycle of motivation and accomplishment. As we become more productive and efficient, we create space for new opportunities and experiences that contribute to our personal and professional growth.

Procrastination is a significant obstacle to personal growth and fulfillment, but it is not insurmountable. By understanding its roots and employing effective strategies to overcome it, we can reclaim our time and unlock our potential. Embracing the power of now and taking immediate action can transform our lives, turning procrastination into productivity and self-doubt into self-growth.

The journey to overcoming procrastination is not always easy, but it is immensely rewarding. Each step forward brings us closer to our goals and dreams, allowing us to live a life of purpose and achievement. So, seize the moment, embrace the present, and let the power of now guide you towards a brighter, more fulfilling future.

CHAPTER TWENTY

Becoming Your Best Self: Radiate Confidence

Confidence is not just an admirable trait; it's a cornerstone of personal growth and success. When we radiate confidence, we empower ourselves to take on challenges, embrace opportunities, and navigate the complexities of life with grace and determination. Building self-esteem is crucial to this process, as it transforms self-doubt into self-growth. Let's explore how boosting self-esteem can help us become our best selves, and the methods to achieve and maintain a confident, growth-oriented mindset.

Understanding Self-Esteem and Confidence

Self-esteem is the perception we have of our own worth. It's our internal gauge of how much we value ourselves, and it profoundly influences our thoughts, behaviors, and interactions. Confidence, on the other hand, is the outward expression of this inner belief. When our self-esteem is high, we exude confidence, which helps us tackle life's challenges and pursue our goals with vigor.

The Impact of Low Self-Esteem

Inhibiting self-worth can hinder one's journey towards personal development. It feeds into a cycle of self-doubt, negative self-talk, and fear of failure. This mindset can prevent us from taking risks, trying new things, or asserting ourselves in personal and professional situations. Over time, low self-esteem can lead to missed opportunities, unfulfilled potential, and a pervasive sense of inadequacy.

Methods to Boost Self-Esteem

1. Practice Self-Compassion

Self-compassion means extending to ourselves the same empathy and care we readily give to our closest friends. It means acknowledging our mistakes and shortcomings without harsh judgment. By practicing self-compassion, we can break the cycle of negative self-talk and cultivate a more supportive inner dialogue. This shift helps build a solid foundation of self-worth and resilience.

2. Set and Achieve Small Goals

Setting and achieving small, manageable goals can provide a significant boost to our self-esteem. Each accomplishment, no matter how minor, reinforces our belief in our abilities and builds momentum for larger successes. Start with simple tasks that align with your interests and values, and gradually increase the complexity as your confidence grows.

3. Embrace Positive Affirmations

Positive affirmations wield significant power in reshaping our subconscious thought patterns. By regularly repeating affirmations that reflect our desired state of being, we can shift our mindset from one of doubt to one of confidence. Phrases like "I am capable," "I deserve success," and "I believe in myself" can help reinforce a positive self-image and combat negative thoughts.

4. Surround Yourself with Supportive People

The people we interact with significantly impact our self-esteem. Surround yourself with individuals who uplift, support, and inspire you. Engage with friends, family, or mentors who believe in your potential and encourage your growth. Limit exposure to those who bring negativity or undermine your confidence.

5. Develop a Growth Mindset

A growth mindset, as defined by psychologist Carol Dweck, is the belief that abilities and intelligence can be developed through effort and perseverance. Embracing a growth mindset helps us view challenges as opportunities for learning rather than threats to our self-worth. This perspective fosters resilience and a proactive approach to personal development.

6. Take Care of Your Physical Well-Being

Physical health is closely linked to mental and emotional well-being. Regular exercise, a balanced diet, and adequate sleep can significantly improve our mood, energy levels, and overall sense of self. When we feel good physically, it's easier to maintain a positive outlook and confidence in our abilities.

7. Celebrate Your Achievements

Taking time to celebrate your achievements, no matter how small, is crucial for building self-esteem. Recognize your achievements and celebrate the efforts you've invested in yourself. This practice reinforces a positive self-image and motivates you to continue striving towards your goals.

8. Challenge Negative Thoughts

Negative thoughts are often automatic and deeply ingrained, but they can be challenged and reframed. When you catch yourself thinking negatively, pause and examine the thought. Ask yourself if it's based on facts or assumptions, and try to reframe it in a more positive or realistic light. Over time, this practice can weaken the hold of negative thinking patterns and strengthen your confidence.

9. Learn New Skills

Learning new skills can be a powerful way to boost self-esteem. It demonstrates our ability to grow and adapt, and it provides tangible evidence of our competence. Whether it's picking up a new hobby, taking a course, or improving a professional skill, continuous learning fosters a sense of accomplishment and self-assurance.

10. Practice Gratitude

Gratitude guides us to see abundance in what we possess rather than scarcity in what we do not. By regularly reflecting on the positive aspects of our lives and expressing gratitude, we cultivate a more positive and appreciative mindset. This practice can enhance our overall sense of well-being and reinforce a positive self-image.

Renovating Self-Doubt into Growth

Building self-esteem is a transformative process that gradually erodes self-doubt and replaces it with confidence and self-belief. As we boost our self-esteem, we begin to see ourselves in a new light—one that is capable, deserving, and full of potential. This transformation opens up new avenues for personal and professional growth.

Overcoming Fear of Failure

One of the most significant barriers to growth is the fear of failure. When we lack confidence, this fear can be paralyzing. However, as we build our self-esteem, we develop the resilience to face challenges head-on. We learn to view failures as learning experiences rather than reflections of our worth. This shift enables us to take risks, pursue new opportunities, and push beyond our comfort zones.

Enhancing Relationships

Confidence also enhances our relationships. When we believe in ourselves, we communicate more effectively, assert our needs and boundaries, and engage more authentically with others. Healthy self-esteem allows us to form deeper connections and build supportive networks that further our personal and professional growth.

Achieving Goals

High self-esteem is a powerful motivator. When we believe in our abilities, we are more likely to set ambitious goals and pursue them with determination. This drive propels us forward, helping us overcome obstacles and achieve success. As we reach our goals, our confidence grows, creating a positive feedback loop that fuels ongoing personal development.

Embracing Authenticity

Confidence allows us to embrace our authentic selves. When we are secure in our worth, we feel free to express our true thoughts, feelings, and desires without fear of judgment or rejection. This authenticity is not only liberating but also attracts opportunities and relationships that align with our true selves, furthering our growth and fulfillment.

Radiating confidence is about more than just feeling good about ourselves; it's about unlocking our full potential and embracing a life of growth and fulfillment. By boosting our self-esteem through self-compassion, goal-setting, positive affirmations, supportive relationships, and other techniques, we can transform self-doubt into a powerful force for personal development.

As we cultivate confidence, we open the door to new possibilities and experiences. We become resilient in the face of challenges, assertive in our pursuits, and authentic in our interactions. The journey to becoming our best selves is not always easy, but it is profoundly rewarding. By embracing our worth and radiating confidence, we can create a life that reflects our true potential and dreams. So, take the first step today—believe in yourself, boost your self-esteem, and watch as your life transforms in ways you never imagined possible.

CHAPTER TWENTY-ONE

CONSIS-TEN-KEY!

Consis-ten-key: Consistency is the Key. Consistency is not merely a virtue; it's the cornerstone of personal growth and transformation. When applied to self-introspection techniques, consistency becomes a powerful tool for uncovering and addressing self-doubt, paving the way for profound self-discovery and growth. This chapter explores the benefits of practicing self-introspection consistently, how it can resurface self-doubt as an opportunity for growth, and why maintaining this practice is crucial for sustained personal development.

The Role of Consistency

Consistency in self-introspection is about making it a regular practice rather than a sporadic event. Just as physical exercise yields greater benefits when done consistently, self-introspection requires ongoing effort to yield meaningful results. By dedicating time and effort consistently, we create space for deep reflection and self-awareness to flourish.

Resurfacing Self-Doubt

Practicing self-introspection consistently may resurface lingering self-doubt or unresolved issues. This process can initially be uncomfortable as it brings to light aspects of ourselves that we may prefer to ignore or suppress. However, confronting these doubts and uncertainties is essential for personal growth. It allows us to address underlying fears, insecurities, or negative beliefs that may be hindering our progress.

Spinning Self-Doubt into Growth

Self-introspection offers an opportunity to transform self-doubt into personal growth. By acknowledging and understanding our doubts, we can begin to challenge them with compassion and curiosity. This process involves reframing negative thoughts, replacing self-limiting beliefs with empowering ones, and taking proactive steps towards self-improvement.

Continuous Process of Growth

Personal growth unfolds as an ongoing journey rather than a final destination. Consistency in self-introspection ensures that we remain committed to this journey of self-discovery and improvement. It allows us to track our progress, learn from setbacks, and adapt our strategies as we evolve.

Benefits of Consistent Self-Introspection

1. **Enhanced Self-Awareness:** Consistent self-introspection deepens our understanding of ourselves, including our strengths, weaknesses, and motivations. This heightened self-awareness enables us to make more informed decisions and align our actions with our values and goals.

2. **Improved Emotional Resilience:** Regular self-introspection strengthens our emotional resilience by helping us identify and manage negative emotions effectively. It equips us with coping strategies and emotional regulation techniques that promote mental well-being.

3. **Clarity of Purpose:** Through consistent self-introspection, we clarify our values, aspirations, and purpose in life. This clarity enables us to set meaningful goals and pursue them with clarity and determination.

4. **Enhanced Problem-Solving Skills:** Self-introspection fosters critical thinking and problem-solving skills. By analyzing past experiences and patterns, we develop insights that guide us in overcoming challenges and making sound decisions.

5. **Strengthened Relationships:** Understanding ourselves better through self-introspection enhances our relationships with others. It improves our communication skills, empathy, and ability to connect authentically with those around us.

Consistency in self-introspection may face challenges such as time constraints, resistance to facing uncomfortable truths, or difficulty maintaining motivation. To overcome these challenges, prioritize self-introspection as a non-negotiable part of your routine, cultivate self-compassion to navigate discomfort, and draw motivation from the tangible benefits of personal growth. Consistency in self-introspection is the key to unlocking our potential, overcoming self-doubt, and achieving sustained personal growth. By committing to this practice, we cultivate greater self-awareness, resilience, clarity of purpose, and enhanced problem-solving skills. Embrace the journey of self-discovery with an open heart and mind, knowing that every moment of introspection brings you closer to becoming your best self. Remember, it's not about perfection but progress, and each step forward enriches your life and contributes to your ongoing evolution.

CHAPTER TWENTY-TWO

The Ocean of Me: Beneath the Surface

I was once a girl who questioned herself too much about every action. There were countless moments when I dismissed my own ideas, fearing what people would say. I was mired in self-doubt, constantly seeking others' approval. "Does this look good on me?" "Am I doing the right thing?" were questions that often escaped my lips. While some saw me as a people pleaser, it was my empathy and kindness driving my actions. I prioritized others over myself, always there for family and friends, offering a shoulder to cry on, an ear to listen, or whatever they needed. Though this trait is still a part of me, I no longer do it at the expense of my own well-being. I help people, but not at the cost of diminishing my self-worth.

I didn't even realize when my introspection journey began. It was a gradual process that helped me understand I am an empath and an extremist, often sacrificing myself to help others. But I also realized that people are self-sufficient; they can help themselves. They simply find alternatives in others. Sometimes, people just need someone to be present during their hardships without offering advice. Other times, they need help to realize their own worth.

This introspection led me to a journey of self-love. I started loving my imperfections, understanding there is no such thing as perfection. Loving my imperfections doesn't mean being rigid; I am open to change. I see myself not as a masterpiece but as a work in progress, a fine art evolving every day. Each day, I open a window for improvement and begin with gratitude for what I have.

During this journey, I also delved into my spiritual depths. I began accepting that the events in my life happen for a reason and serve a greater purpose. I started approaching life with a positive and optimistic outlook, trusting that the universe's actions are for our own good. I realized I am not answerable or accountable for others' words and actions. I am accountable for my behavior and efforts in life. I should always do my part without worrying about others. I am responsible for my words, mood, and actions, and temporary discomforts should not lead me to surrender to negative emotions or become unreasonable. I began setting goals and challenges, often surpassing my expectations and surprising myself in the process. One such challenge was my 30-day writing endeavor.

I was always in denial, thinking I had no expectations from anyone. But through introspection, I discovered I do have certain expectations from myself and my loved ones. I learned it's normal to have expectations, but they should not compromise my core values.

I am skilled in the art of listening attentively and observing keenly. I remember nine out of ten things anyone shares with me. During this journey, I started being vocal about my emotions. I used to be very secretive, thinking my emotions were trivial and that sharing them would burden others. But I realized that everyone should have a human diary; it's essential. There was a day when I was at my most vulnerable phase and called all my safe people one by one. Some didn't answer, while others said they were busy and would call back but never did. In the past, I would have kept quiet about the situation. But this time, I spoke up and made them realize I had expectations—not necessarily to provide advice, but to be present with me and distract me from my vulnerability. I wasn't complaining; I was signaling that I needed support. My friends immediately created a safe word to address such situations in the future. This proactive step showed the importance of communicating our needs. If I had stayed silent, I would have been burdened by the belief that no one was there for me when I needed them.

Being an over thinker made this process both easy and challenging. I was already using many techniques to manage overthinking, but what I lacked were boundaries. I won't say I have reached the pinnacle of introspection or completely transformed my self-doubt into growth. No, that's not the case. This journey is evocative and infinite; as self-doubts will surface throughout life. However, being a quick learner, I have developed the right techniques to transform these doubts into pillars of growth.

Introspection holds all the lessons we need; the art of living is within ourselves. We must give ourselves the pen to write our remarkable story.

The knowledge within us is abundant. What we need is the right perspective and purpose. We must be open to gathering more information and be willing to refine ourselves through consistent effort and application. This is the key to success.

In the professional world, there is a term called "employable." In life, the equivalent is "lovable." Believe that all creatures in the world are lovable, and we need to cultivate this vision within ourselves. This journey of introspection and transformation has taught me that while helping others is important, maintaining my self-worth and growth is equally crucial. I am a work in progress, evolving each day with gratitude, self-love, and a positive outlook in life.

Books By The Author

Eternal Love: Can Happen Twice?

-By Chitra Jaiswal

In this collection of 22 poignant poems, titled "Eternal Love - Can Happen Twice?" we embark on a journey of exploration and introspection. Love, often considered a once-in-a-lifetime experience, is believed to be unique and irreplaceable. But is it truly confined to just one occurrence? Can the heart find its way to love again, even after enduring the heartache of loss?

From Foes to Flames

-By Chitra Jaiswal

In the vast tapestry of human emotions, few threads are as intricate and entangled as the journey from rivalry to romance. "From Foes to Flames" unravels the story of two individuals whose destinies are interwoven in the most unexpected of ways

Shades in Pairs: Tangled Threads of Life

-By Chitra Jaiswal

In the murky realm where shadows dance with secrets, "Shades in Pairs: Tangled Threads of Life" unravels a web of suspense that binds the destinies of unsuspecting souls. As the threads of the ordinary intertwine with the extraordinary, the boundaries between light and darkness blur, revealing a tapestry of intrigue. Brace yourself for a journey through clandestine alleys, where every step echoes with the heartbeat of a hidden truth, and where the chilling resonance of paired shades heralds the enigma that lies ahead.

The Echoing Algorithm

By Chitra Jaiswal

Dive into the chilling depths of 'The Echoing Algorithm,' where reality twists and shadows dance. Unravel the mysteries of a haunted algorithm that echoes with supernatural whispers. As darkness encroaches, a spine-tingling journey unfolds, blurring the lines between the digital and the supernatural. Brace yourself for a riveting tale that will haunt your thoughts long after the last page.

Thank You

Thank you, dear readers, for embarking on the transformative journey through the pages of "Unearth 21 Techniques to Transform Self-Doubts to Growth: Dive Deep into the Ocean of Introspection." Your willingness to explore the depths of self-reflection and personal growth is truly inspiring. Each page turned, each technique practiced, and each moment of introspection has made this journey vibrant and meaningful.

Your courage to face self-doubts head-on and your commitment to fostering growth within yourself have breathed life into this book. I am deeply grateful for your engagement, and I hope the insights and exercises within these pages continue to resonate with you, guiding you towards a more confident and empowered self.

May the lessons learned and the reflections made accompany you on your path to self-discovery. Your presence in this shared journey adds profound depth to the collective experience of growth and transformation. Until our paths cross again, may you continue to dive deep, unearthing the treasures of your true potential.

www.ingramcontent.com/pod-product-compliance
Lightning Source LLC
LaVergne TN
LVHW021200160826
845679LV00024B/2182

* 9 7 9 8 8 9 4 7 5 2 2 2 8 *